LATVIAN CHILDREN'S BOOK

The Wonderful Wizard of Oz

WAI CHEUNG

©Copyright, 2017, by Wai Cheung and Maestro Publishing Group
All rights reserved.

No part of this book may be reproduced or transmitted in any form or by any means, electronic or mechanical, including photocopying, recording or by any information storage and retrieval system, without permission in writing of the copyright owner.

Printed in the United States of America.

ABOUT THE BOOK

Raise your children in a bilingual fashion with this bilingual coloring book that captures the magic and beauty of Wizard of Oz's story along with a dual language storytelling that is perfect for parents who want to raise their children in a bilingual environment.

CONTENTS

Plate 1 3

Plate 2 5

Plate 3 7

Plate 4 9

Plate 5 11

Plate 6 13

Plate 7 15

Plate 8 17

This page intentionally left blank.

Dorothy Gale, who lived in Kansas with her Uncle Henry, Aunt Em and her little dog Toto, found herself nearly swept away by a large tornado.

Dorotija Geila, kura dzīvo Kanzasā kopā ar savu tēvoci Henriju, tanti Emu un savu mazo suņuku Toto, attopas pēc tam, kad viņu teju no zemes virsas noslaucījusi varena viesuļvētra.

Plate 1

The tornado picked up the entire house with Dorothy and Toto in it and deposited them in a land where Munchkins greeted them with joy.

Spēcīgā vētra parauj līdzi visu māju kopā ar Dorotiju un Toto, nogādājot tos kādā zemē, kur viņus laipni sveic mazie ļautiņi gremoņi.

Plate 2

The Good Witch of the North told Dorothy that in order to return home, she must see the Wizard of Oz in the Emerald City, and she gave the girl a pair of magical Silver Shoes.

Labā Ziemeļu ragana Dorotijai izstāsta, ka, lai atgrieztos mājās, viņai Smaragda pilsētā jāsatiek Ozas burvis, un dāvā meitenei maģiskās Sudraba kurpes.

Plate 3

Along the way, Dorothy met three new friends: The Scarecrow, The Tin Woodman and the Cowardly Lion.

Ceļā Dorotija satiek trīs jaunus draugus: Putnubiedēkli, Dzelzs Malkascirtēju un Bailīgo Lauvu.

Plate 4

Dorothy and her new friends made it to the Emerald City, where the Wizard gave them all the same mission: Destroy the Wicked Witch of the West.

Dorotija kopā ar saviem jaunajiem draugiem nokļūst Smaragda pilsētā, kur Burvis visiem uzdod vienu misiju: iznīcināt Ļauno Rietumu raganu.

Plate 5

The Wicked Witch finally captured Dorothy and made her a personal slave, all while attempting to steal the Silver Shoes.

Ļaunā ragana visbeidzot notver Dorotiju un paverdzina viņu, vienlaikus mēģinot nozagt Sudraba kurpes.

Plate 6

The Wicked Witch got one shoe from Dorothy, but the young girl became so angry she picked up the bucket and tossed the water on the witch — who, to her surprise, melted!

Ļaunajai raganai izdodas no Dorotijas iegūt vienu kurpi, taču jaunā meitene tik ļoti sadusmojas, ka ņem spaini ar ūdeni un uzlej to raganai – kura, viņai par pārsteigumu, izkūst!

Plate 7

Jubilant, Dorothy and her friends returned to the Emerald City, and Glinda, the Good Witch of the South, showed her how to return to Kansas: click her heels together three times and wish for home.

Dorotija un viņas draugi līksmodami atgriežas Smaragda pilsētā, un Glinda, Labā Dienvidu ragana, parāda viņai, kā atgriezties Kanzasā: tris reizes jāsasit kopā papēži un jāievēlas nokļūt mājās.

Plate 8

This page intentionally left blank.

ABOUT THE BOOK

Raise your children in a bilingual fashion with this bilingual coloring book that captures the magic and beauty of Wizard of Oz's story along with a dual language storytelling that is perfect for parents who want to raise their children in a bilingual environment.

Made in the USA
Columbia, SC
28 September 2022